Mercury

Ray Spangenburg and Kit Moser

Franklin Watts
A Division of Scholastic Inc.
New York • Toronto • London • Auckland • Sydney
Mexico City • New Delhi • Hong Kong
Danbury, Connecticut

Note to readers: Definitions for words in **bold** can be found in the Glossary at the back of this book.

Photographs ©: Corbis-Bettmann: 10, 16; ESA: 51; Finley-Holiday Films: 3 top, 9; Mark Robinson: 38; NASA: 44, 45 (colored by Mehau Kulyk/SPL), 31 (JPL), cover, 18, 19, 22, 24, 25, 29, 34, 41 top, 49; Osservatorio Astonomico di Brera: 12; Photo Researchers, NY: 52 (Chris Butler/SPL), 36 (Lynette Cook/SPL), 7 (John Foster/SS), 4 (David A. Hardy/SPL), 33 right (Royal Observatory, Edinburgh/SPL), 46 (US Geological Survey/ SPL), 41 bottom (Charles D. Winters/Timeframe Photography Inc.); Photri: 3, 21, 26, 27, 33 left, 42.

Solar system diagram created by Greg Harris

Library of Congress Cataloging-in-Publication Data

Spangenburg, Ray, 1939–
    Mercury/ Ray Spangenburg and Kit Moser.
        p.   cm.— (Watts Library)
    Includes bibliographical references and index.
    Summary: Describes the orbit, temperature, surface formations, composition, and theories of formation of the planet Mercury, and the probe *Mariner 10* that took pictures of it in 1974 and 1975.
    ISBN: 0-531-11766-9 (lib. bdg.)   0-531-13986-7 (pbk.)
    1. Mercury (Planet)—Juvenile literature. [1. Mercury (Planet)] I. Moser, Diane, 1944– II. Title.III. Series.
QB611 .S63 2001
523.41—dc21   00-038201

Contents

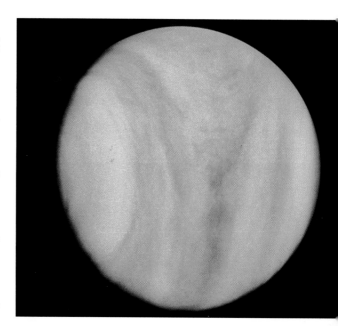

This artwork shows how close Mercury travels to the Sun.

Chapter One

Sun-Baked Rock

Mercury is the second smallest planet and the planet nearest the Sun. This small, sun-scorched world has practically no air, no water, and no moon. It is very hard to see from Earth because it orbits so close to the Sun. In the past, it was possible to see Mercury only during twilight, right before sunset or right before sunrise. People watched Mercury rise and set more than four thousand years ago, but no one knew much about Mercury then.

Mercury moves very fast—so fast it is sometimes known as the "quick planet." The ancient Romans named the planet Mercury, after one of the Roman gods. According to Roman mythology, Mercury wore wings on his hat and sandals as he carried messages to the gods. Mercury was known for his speed.

How Did the Planets Form?

When the solar system started out about 4.6 billion years ago, it was just a huge cloud of hot gases and dust. This cloud is often called the **solar nebula**, or the "Sun's cloud," because the star we call the Sun formed at its center. As the Sun formed, the hot **mass** of gases and dust swirled around it in the shape of a flattened, circular disk. Slowly this orbiting disk began to cool off. The gases turned into solids, and this material began to stick together, forming larger and larger objects. These objects became what we now know as planets, moons, **comets, asteroids**, and **meteoroids**—all orbiting the Sun.

During the first few billion years after the Sun formed, the solar system was chaotic. Chunks of rock crossed paths with planets, moons, asteroids, and comets. Sometimes these rocks

would crash into one another and shatter into billions of pieces. Sometimes they smashed into planets or moons and combined with them. Some scientists call this period the "great bombardment." The planet Mercury and Earth's Moon still show the deep scars of this period.

The solar system's planets and other objects took shape out of a huge disk of hot gases and dust that swirled around the newly formed Sun.

Moving Planets

Planets move in two different ways. They spin like tops, or **rotate**. One spin is called a rotation. They also travel around the Sun in a path called an **orbit**. One trip around the Sun is called a **revolution**. Mercury's path around the Sun is a flattened oval, much longer than it is wide. This is called an eccentric orbit.

Reading Mercury's Past

Like the Moon, Mercury is one of the solar system's terrestrial bodies. The surfaces of these rocky worlds show many events that have taken place since they formed. Erupting volcanoes spread hot lava over a surface. Meteorites crash into it. These events leave behind a visible history and destroy parts of the previous record. Geologists use these clues on the surface to read a planet's history.

Birth of Mercury

Only certain minerals that could withstand its intense heat could exist in the area close to the Sun. Those few minerals, such as iron and basaltic silicates, grouped together to form Mercury. The amount of material was small, so the planet had only a weak gravitational pull. Lighter materials escaped or were boiled away by the intense heat of the Sun. Nearly all gases disappeared, leaving Mercury airless. Since the planet had almost no air pressure, any water that formed evaporated immediately. No small object formed to orbit Mercury as its moon.

Recently, though, some scientists have suggested that Mercury may have formed in other interesting ways. A Russian scientist suggested in 1991 that Mercury may once have been a moon of Venus. Then, a passing asteroid crashed into Mercury, knocking it away from Venus and into a new orbit around the Sun. This scenario would explain why both Mercury and Venus are moonless.

The View from Mercury

If you could transport yourself to Mercury and stand on its surface, you would be three times closer to the Sun than a person standing on Earth. The Sun would look three times bigger from Mercury. You might see two other objects that are not as large or as bright as the Sun. They might look a lot like very bright stars. Those objects would be the two closest planets—Venus and Earth. Venus would be the brighter of

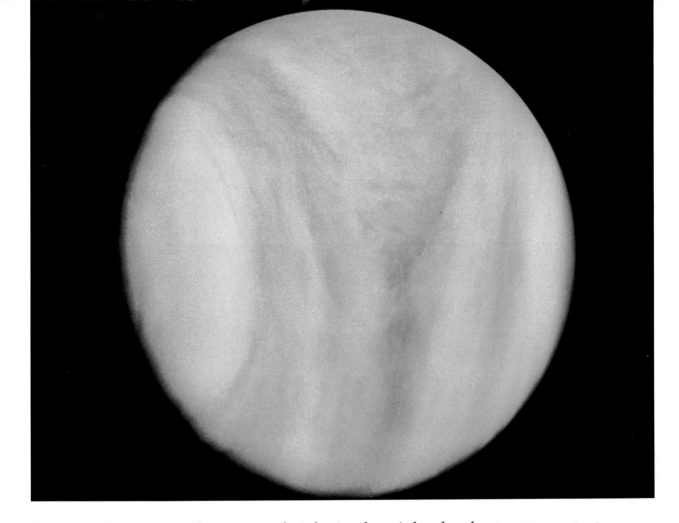

the two. Sometimes they are so bright in the night sky that they cast faint shadows on Mercury's surface.

Venus is the closest planet to Mercury.

If you traveled from the daytime side of Mercury to the nighttime side of Mercury, you would notice an extreme change in temperature. The side of Mercury facing the Sun would be very hot, with temperatures as high as 800 degrees Fahrenheit (427 degrees Celsius). At the same time, the nighttime side would be extremely cold, with temperatures as low as –279°F (–173°C). This unique characteristic is one of many that have captured the interest of scientists.

Giovanni Schiaparelli (1835–1910) used a telescope to make a map of Mercury. The job took him 8 years.

Chapter Two

Exploring Mercury

Mercury has always been difficult to see and a challenge to learn about. By the late 1800s, though, telescopes were powerful enough to give astronomers a closer look. From 1881 to 1889, the Italian astronomer Giovanni Schiaparelli made the first attempt to map Mercury's surface using a telescope. When Giovanni Schiaparelli was 25 years old, he became the director of Brera Observatory in Milan, Italy. He spent the next 40 years studying the solar system—including the planets, their moons, the comets, and asteroids. While Schiaparelli was peering through his telescope at Mars in 1877, he thought he saw a series of long, straight lines. He called them "canali," which means "channels" in Italian. English-speaking astronomers misunderstood him, though. They thought he was saying he had seen *canals*—like the waterways people have built on Earth!

That's not all. Schiaparelli also saw some streaks on the surface of Mercury. Were these canals too? This was hard for some people to believe, because Mercury is so close to the Sun's intense heat. Today, we know there is no running water on either Mars or Mercury, and no long, straight channels. The canals were an optical illusion. Another mapmaker,

Schiaparelli became director of Brera Observatory in Milan, Italy.

Eugenios Antoniadi (1870–1944) had a much better telescope to work with. He could see there were definitely no canals and he published his map of Mercury in 1934.

Getting the details right about Mercury was still difficult, though. From their observations, both Antoniadi and Schiaparelli thought that Mercury rotated, or turned on its **axis**, once for every orbit it made around the Sun. They thought that Mercury was locked into motions that kept one side always facing the bright heat of the Sun. The other side, they thought, was always dark and cold. Then, scientists received some new information. Some studies using microwaves in the early 1960s showed that the side of Mercury facing away from the Sun was hot. This was a big surprise. Researchers began to suspect that Mercury spins faster than anyone had thought. In 1965, scientists used radar to study Mercury's rotation. They discovered that Mercury rotates three times in every two trips around the Sun. So there is no part of Mercury that stays dark and cold. The Sun shines on each part of Mercury once every 176 days.

Pinging a Planet

Using radar, scientists could detect Mercury's features and time the planet's rotation. Radar can also be used to make maps. Radar mapping works by sending out a microwave, or radar, signal from a transmitter in the spacecraft. The signal bounces off the surface of the planet, and then the spacecraft accurately times the bounced signal's round trip. This measurement helps scientists to understand what the distant surface looks like.

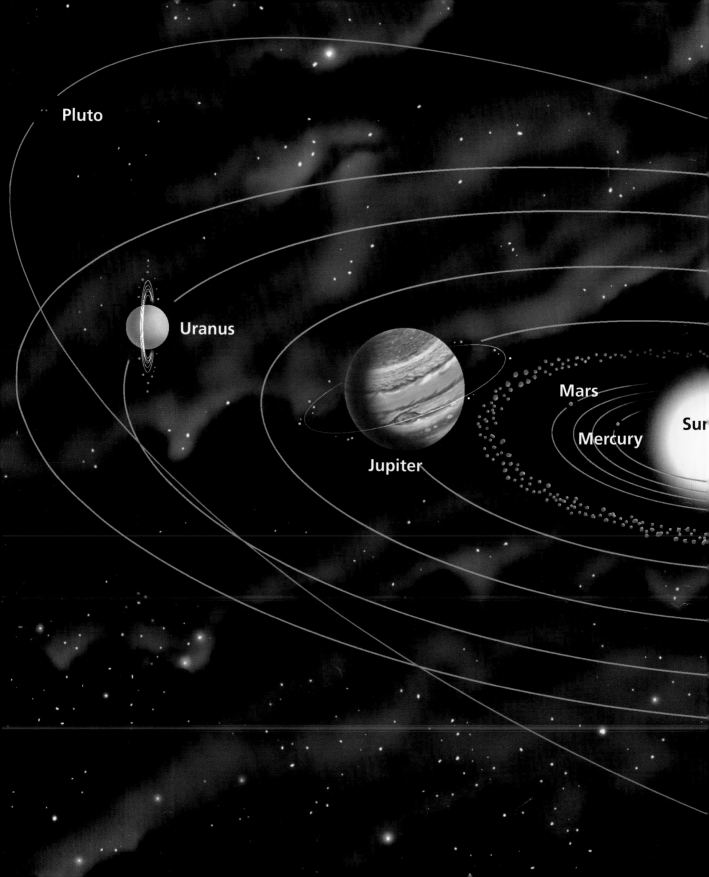

The Solar System

Venus

Moon

Earth

Asteroid Belt

Saturn

Neptune

Strange Journey

Mercury traces a long, oval path around the Sun, so the planet is not always the same distance from the Sun. It can be as close as 29 million miles (47 million km), and as far away as 44 million miles (71 million km) from the Sun. Mercury's total trip around the Sun takes 88 days.

Suppose you were standing on Mercury watching the Sun. Given the planet's **elliptical** orbit and its slow rotation, the Sun would seem to travel strangely across the planet's black,

Vulcan, the Missing Planet

In the mid-1800s, a French astronomer named Urbain Leverrier looked at the effect one planet has on the orbit of another planet. His calculations predicted the existence of Neptune before anyone knew it was there.

Later, Leverrier saw a similar effect in Mercury's orbit. He thought another planet might be located between Mercury and the Sun. One amateur astronomer even wrote Leverrier that he thought he saw this missing planet. Leverrier named the planet Vulcan, after the Roman god of fire. Astronomers have searched for years for Vulcan, but no one has found solid evidence of its existence. Most "sightings" were probably just sunspots, or a comet passing close to the Sun.

airless sky. In some locations, you would see the Sun travel partway across the sky, seem to stop, and then trace a loop overhead. In other locations, you might see the Sun rise in the east, set soon afterward, and then rise again and start across the sky. At sunset, it would set, rise shortly afterward, and finally set again!

Visitor from Earth

In 1974 and 1975, a spacecraft named *Mariner 10* gave planetary scientists—and the rest of the world—a chance to take a much closer look at the surface of Mercury. *Mariner 10* was launched by NASA in 1973—the first and only spacecraft to make the voyage to the tiny innermost planet.

When NASA scientists first began planning the *Mariner 10* mission, they had planned on flying by Venus. Then they realized that a few small adjustments would allow a very unusual flight path past Mercury. *Mariner 10* was the first to use what NASA calls a "gravity assist." **Gravity** is the force that pulls an object toward the center of a planet or other body in space. As *Mariner 10* neared Venus, it used Venus's gravitational pull to give it a boost. The boost bent *Mariner 10*'s path and speeded the little spacecraft up to send it on to Mercury. Space scientists have used this trick many times since the 1970s to make the most of a spacecraft's journey.

Then mission scientists realized that a gravity assist could also be used to arrange a bonus. Because Mercury orbits the Sun in a unique way, *Mariner 10* was able to make one trip

Mariner 10 made NASA's first dual planet mission. The spacecraft visited both Venus and Mercury.

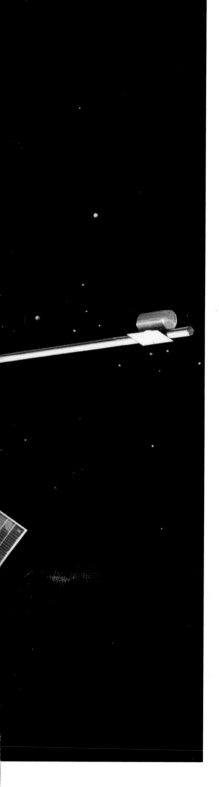

around the Sun and encounter Mercury three times! This was a great opportunity for the very first close-up looks at the planet nearest the Sun.

Next Stop: Mercury

The spacecraft first approached Mercury on March 29, 1974. It passed very close to the planet, within 438 miles (705 kilometers). As *Mariner 10* made its first pass by Mercury, scientists made several surprising discoveries. First, using a special instrument called a **magnetometer**, they were able to see that Mercury had a magnetic field! That means that Mercury, like Earth, has a magnetic north pole and a magnetic south pole. Mercury's magnetic field is the region influenced by the pull of the magnetic poles. Scientists had not expected to make this discovery because Mercury rotates much more slowly on its axis than Earth. This slow movement did not seem to provide enough force to create a magnetic field. The second big surprise from the first flyby was the discovery of Mercury's **atmosphere**—a body of gases around the planet. *Mariner 10* used an instrument called an ultraviolet (UV) spectrometer to detect the elements present on Mercury. Each element, such as iron, carbon, and so on, displays a unique characteristic that the spectrometer can recognize. When scientists saw the characteristic of the gas helium, they knew they had discovered an atmosphere. This was amazing. Because Mercury is so close to the Sun, scientists thought its heat would have boiled away all the planet's gases long ago. Of course, Mercury's atmosphere was extremely thin—only one-billionth the density of Earth's atmosphere. The third surprise was that Mercury's **crust** proved to be light in weight. From Earth-based observations, scientists already knew that Mercury was nearly as dense as Earth, so the lightweight crust was unexpected too.

For the first time, observers realized that Mercury was covered with wide, shallow basins that looked a lot like the **craters** found on the Moon and Mars. *Mariner 10* transmitted about 2,000 photos of Mercury back to Earth. The photos

This image shows the craters on Mercury's surface.

Over 200 Mariner 10 *photographs make up this mosaic looking down on the south pole (midpoint at bottom of picture).*

were clear enough to show craters as small as 100 miles (161 km) across. Unfortunately, the closest brush made on this pass was on the night side of Mercury—the side unlit by the Sun—so *Mariner 10* couldn't take photographs during that time.

Mariner 10 passed by for the second time on September 21, 1974. This time the spacecraft took a more distant look at Mercury, from 29,871 miles (48,071 km)—a good distance for large-scale mapping. It took photos of the sunlit side of the planet and the region around the south pole. The spacecraft succeeded in mapping 45 percent of the planet's surface.

A Look at Magnetism

On March 16, 1975, *Mariner 10* sped by Mercury for one last look. This time the spacecraft flew at a very low altitude—203 miles (327 km). It took about 300 more photos, but photography was not its main mission on this run. Scientists wanted a closer reading on the planet's magnetic field.

They learned that the magnetic field came from the planet itself—a finding that puzzled many scientists. Until then, scientists thought that a magnetic field was created by a planet's rotation and the fluid movement of its molten iron **core**. And Mercury did not seem to rotate fast enough. So what created its magnetism? This question has still not been answered.

On March 25, 1975, *Mariner 10* ran out of the gas it needed for controlling its altitude, and NASA scientists had to end the mission. No spacecraft has ever gone back to Mercury to find out more. As a result, some people call Mercury "the forgotten planet." Many scientists believe they could learn a lot about the solar system and the formation of planets by exploring Mercury further.

Cold at the Poles?

Since 1975, scientists have added a few Earth-based observations to *Mariner 10*'s stunning findings. In 1991,

Mercury's south pole is located inside the deeply shadowed crater at the lower center of this photo. Craters like this one may provide a permanent deep freeze where deposits of ice may exist.

researchers bounced radar off Mercury to find out more about the terrain, and they came up with a real surprise. Small areas showed unusual radar reflections. In spite of Mercury's great heat, this evidence suggested that small amounts of ice may exist at the poles!

The reflections suggest that ice deposits—small amounts of ice crystals mixed with surface dust and soil—may exist near the poles, away from the Sun's greatest heat. There, comet collisions may have sprayed frozen material into the shade of big rocks or deep craters and crevices. Or water vapor in Mercury's thin atmosphere may have frozen into tiny crystals of ice. The long shadows cast by the Sun in these regions may cause a permanent deep freeze—allowing ice to form.

Of all the objects in the solar system, many scientists think our Moon may be the most similar to Mercury. In 1996, scientists had even more reason to compare these two objects. On our Moon, scientists found similar signs of small water ice deposits hidden deep in craters, away from the Sun's heat. This evidence first turned up in 1996 in data from a mission made in 1994 by a U.S. spacecraft named *Clementine*. In 1998, *Lunar Prospector*, another robot visitor to the Moon, found further evidence of ice in shadowed regions. Many planetary scientists think that studies of our Moon may hold keys to understanding how Mercury formed and what has happened to it since.

This montage of Mercury, taken by Mariner 10, shows the planet's deeply scarred surface.

Chapter Three

Asteroid Target

Before *Mariner 10*'s journey to Mercury, no one knew that the innermost planet's surface was covered with craters. We now know that Mercury has thousands of such scars; meteorites, asteroids, and comets have smashed into it for thousands of years. Most of Mercury has a rough, rugged terrain, dotted with craters, very much like the Moon, Mars, and Jupiter's moon Callisto. A few smooth lava plains exist on Mercury's surface. They were probably formed by

When a small object in space crashes into a larger one, it leaves an impact crater, or saucer-shaped depression, in the surface. When a meteorite smashes into Mercury, the force of the impact breaks up material on the surface, melts it, and ejects it by throwing it upward and outward. Pieces of broken rock and rubble that have shot up may fall back to the surface. When they land, they often create smaller craters around the main crater. The pockmarked face of Mercury tells the story of many, many hits in the past 3 billion years.

molten material long, long ago. No one is quite sure exactly how these plains formed.

A Smashing Good Time

Scientists think that the many craters we see on the surface of Mercury and Earth's Moon were formed long ago in the history of the solar system—during the great bombardment. It was a time when many objects sped across the space between planets and moons and smashed into anything in their path. The large number of ancient craters on Mercury show that many more hits took place in the past than occur today. The surface of Mercury and the Moon look like they had a similar history—heavy bombardment followed by filling with molten lava. Both surfaces have also gone unchanged for billions of years.

When you look at one side of Mercury, you can't help noticing the biggest feature on the surface of this small planet. It is the Caloris Basin, a huge, round, ringed basin with no

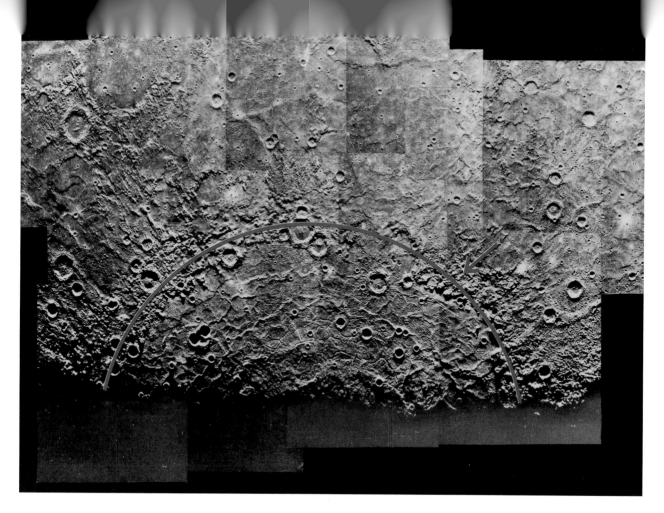

outlet. The basin is 800 miles (1,287 km) across, and it looks a lot like the large, rounded basins found on the Moon. Scientists think an asteroid or comet may have smashed into Mercury early in its history and formed the Caloris Basin. Over time, lava probably filled the deep gash caused by the impact and smoothed it out.

Mariner 10 captured images of about half of Caloris Basin—the part lit by the Sun when the spacecraft passed overhead. The images show the eastern edge, where huge rough blocks 0.6 to 1.2 miles (1 to 2 km) high are thrown up

The large half-circle area at the bottom of this photo, outlined and marked with an arrow, is half of Caloris Basin, the largest feature on the surface of Mercury.

Hot Spot

The name Caloris comes from the Latin word *calor*, meaning "heat." Caloris Basin is one of two hot spots on Mercury's surface that face the Sun directly when the planet orbits closest to the Sun.

along the rim. To the northeast, hills and mountains spread out from the rim like rays of light from the Sun. To the east, lumpy plains stretch out into one of Mercury's mysterious smooth plains.

A series of ridges and fractures along Caloris Basin's smooth basin floor have puzzled scientists. Some believe these features are caused by tectonics—the crumpling of geologic layers or strata caused by sideways pressure. Others insist that volcanic lava flows formed the ridges when molten material pushed up through cracks in the basin floor.

Most scientists agree, however, that a tremendous impact jolted the planet about 3.8 billion years ago. It was the second-largest recorded collision on any of the four rocky planets, caused by a huge, asteroid-like object about 93 miles (150 km) in **diameter**. When this impact took place, the energy released by the explosion was equivalent to a trillion 1-mega-ton hydrogen bombs. The giant impact created Caloris Basin and shock waves rumbled all the way around and through the planet.

Evidence of these massive shock waves showed up on the other side of the planet. There, a region of rough rock and

Rival Crater

Among the inner planets—those closest to the Sun—the only impact crater bigger than the Caloris Basin is the South Pole-Aitken Basin. This huge crater is located on the far side of Earth's Moon and measures 1,616 miles (2,600 km) across.

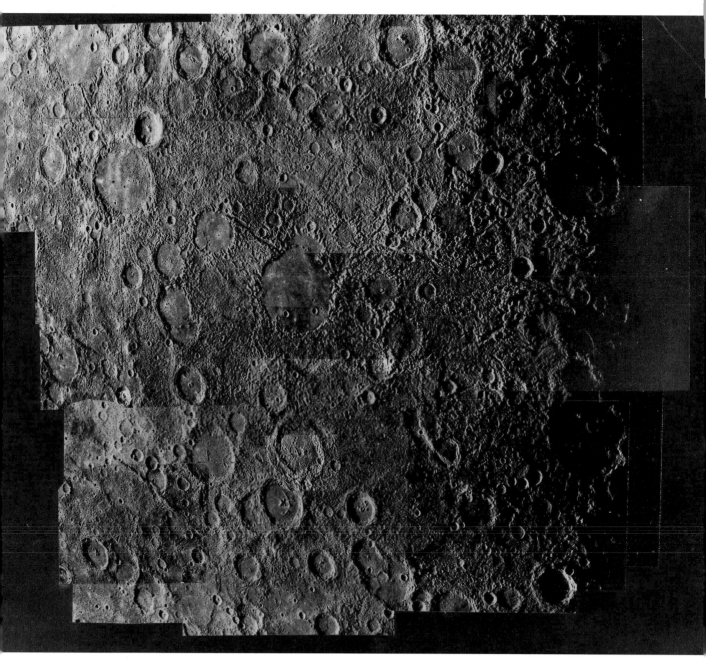

On the other side of the planet from the Caloris Basin impact lies a jumble of rock and crosscutting ridges that is unique to Mercury. This weird terrain may have been caused by shock waves from the giant impact that formed Caloris Basin.

crust breaks up into a chaotic series of jumbled blocks. Scientists describe this hilly, rugged area as "weird terrain" and it does indeed look weird. Experts believe it was formed when the impact at Caloris Basin sent shock waves through the planet's crust as surface waves. At the same time, compression waves passed through the planet's core. Within minutes, all these forces had traveled to the opposite side of the planet where they combined. As a result, ragged hills and valleys were pushed up to cut across the old hills, valleys, and craters. The ground shot upward as much as 0.6 mile (1 km). Deep fractures, or cracks, opened in the planet's crust, and great blocks of material were dislodged. Nothing like this region of chaotic, contorted rubble has been seen anywhere else in the solar system.

Shrinking Skin and Crumbling Dust

In another part of Mercury, *Mariner 10* discovered enormous cliffs that cut across surface craters as if the brittle rock had shattered like glass. These cliffs were created billions of years ago, as the early planet cooled and shrank. The planet's skin contracted and shriveled, causing enormous pressure. As this internal pressure built up, one huge block of crust would rise up. Meanwhile, the block next to it sank. These cliffs cut across mountains, valleys, and craters. They extend for hundreds of miles—up to 310 miles (499 km) long. Some tower up to 13,000 ft (3,962 meters) high, nearly as high as Hawaii's biggest mountain, Mauna Kea.

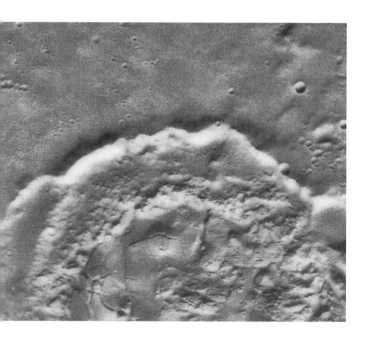

Mercury's terrain is covered with dust, caused by billions of years of pummeling by the chips off asteroids, meteorites, and comets that scientists call "micrometeorites." Another force, called **thermal** erosion, creates even more dust. Between daytime and nighttime, the large temperature swings of nearly 1100° F (593° C) cause the rocks to expand with the heat and contract with the cold. This continual expansion and shrinking of Mercury's surface causes pieces of rock to chip off and crumble to dust.

Some ridges and cliffs on Mercury (left) tower nearly as high as Mauna Kea (right) in Hawaii.

"Dead" Rock

From the condition of the craters, planetary scientists can figure out the age of Mercury's surface. As we have seen, Mercury's surface has many, many craters. Most of them are almost as deep and jagged as the day they formed—when a

Most of the features on Mercury's surface are there to stay—little erosion or other forces are around to change anything.

large rock came whizzing through space and smashed into the planet's surface.

Not much happens on Mercury to change the way these craters look. The planet has no rivers flowing through the craters to wash away the walls. No volcanoes erupt to fill the giant holes with lava and melted rock. And no winds blow to shift the dust and wear away the edges. The erosion on Earth caused by the forces of weather, water, and volcanoes does not exist on Mercury. The only erosion on Mercury's surface is caused by the tiny impacts from thousands of micrometeorites and the expanding and shrinking of its surface.

Scientists have measured the age of the big craters on Mercury, and they can see that they have remained almost untouched by geological activity for billions of years. In geological terms, Mercury has been dead for about 3 to 4 billion years. That's why some scientists call it the "dead rock" close to the Sun.

Is Mercury More Like a Moon or a Planet?

	Mercury	Earth's Moon	Earth
Distance	36 million miles (57.9 million km) from Sun	238,860 miles (384,397 km) from Earth	93 million miles (150 million km) from Sun
One year (complete orbit)	88 Earth-days to orbit the Sun	27.3 Earth-days to orbit Earth	365.25 Earth days to orbit the Sun
One day (complete turn on its axis)	58.6 Earth-days	29.4 Earth-days	1 Earth-day (24 hours)
Diameter	3,032 miles (4,879 km)	2,160 miles (3,476 km)	7,927 miles (12,757 km)
Surface material	Dust and rock	Dust and rock	Water and soil
Surface appearance	Dry and barren, with many craters	Dry and barren, with many craters	Oceans and land-masses; forests and other living things; few craters
Atmosphere	Almost no atmosphere	No atmosphere	Thick atmosphere: 78 percent nitrogen 21 percent oxygen 1 percent water

Seventy-five percent of Mercury's diameter is taken up by its large, iron core.

Chapter Four

Inside Mercury

Scientists are still puzzling over the story of Mercury's interior. On the outside, this small world looks a lot like Earth's Moon. Like the Moon, Mercury is pockmarked by ancient craters and appears to have no internal activity at all. Yet, Mercury seems to have some big differences deep inside. The little planet has a giant core for its size. This core is probably made of iron, and it may be very hot and molten. The Moon, though, has no fluid regions—it is completely solid.

Also, some scientists think that seething, hot lava may once have burst to Mercury's surface from below. By studying *Mariner 10*'s images in new ways, researchers have begun to learn about the planet's interior—what it is made of and what happened there. To study the images, they marked the pictures with different colors for different shapes. Then they matched the patterns of these colors with other information they had about what the surface rocks are made of. What they saw reminded them of surface material from violent volcanic eruptions on Earth and other planets.

Scientists think the light blue areas in this Mariner 10 *image may be ancient volcanoes.*

Iron at the Core

Planets are not just huge chunks of rock traveling around the Sun. They are made up of layers. The surface you see is the outermost layer, the crust. This is the thinnest layer. The second layer, the **mantle**, is usually the largest layer of a planet. At the center is the core. It is usually made of heavier elements that sank to the center when the planet first formed and its material was still hot and molten.

Mercury's interior is odd, though. The outside looks so much like the Moon's—and geologists can see that the history of impacts from other objects is very similar to the Moon's. Yet, not everything is the same, and scientists conclude that part of Mercury's history must have been very different from the Moon's.

Scientists used *Mariner 10*'s interaction with Mercury to get a measurement of the planet's gravity. They found out that even though Mercury's diameter is less than 1-1/2 times bigger than the Moon's, the little planet exerts more than twice as much gravity as the Moon. Its density (a measure of how tightly it is packed) is almost as high as Earth's. Mercury also contains at least twice as much iron as any other planet in the solar system. So, scientists estimate that the core must be very large—taking up to about 65 to 75 percent of the planet.

Mercury, Venus, Earth, and Mars all have a dense core rich in iron. When materials in the mantle melted, lighter materials floated to the surface and solidified. Heavier materials settled to the center, forming a heavy core. What's amazing

Rocky Planet

Mercury is one of the four terrestrial planets, or "rocky planets." This group also includes Venus, Earth, and Mars.

Heavy Metal

Iron is found naturally on Earth as a solid metal. It is silvery white in its pure form and it is naturally magnetic. You can find rocks containing iron (known as iron ore) on Earth's surface. On Mercury, though, almost all the planet's iron is deep inside, within its large core.

about Mercury, though, is that its core is so large, so dense, and so rich in iron. Also, Mercury seems to show very little iron in its surface rock and dust.

Scientists have proposed three different ideas about how Mercury's core developed, but so far no one has good enough evidence to know which one may be right. Perhaps when the planet formed, thin gases from the solar nebula slowed heavier substances enough so they tended to clump together more than lighter substances in Mercury's neighborhood. So, Mercury ended up with more heavy metals, such as iron. At the surface, though, its makeup was much the same as all the other planets—mostly composed of rocks made of a substance called silicate.

Another idea is that early in the planet's development, the tremendous heat of the nearby Sun caused the outer layer of rock to disintigrate. Heat given off by radioactive substances may also have contributed to the furnace that melted Mercury. At that time, the heaviest metals, such as iron, would have sunk to the center to form Mercury's very heavy core. If so, this happened at least 3 to 4 billion years ago. Then finally, when the planet cooled, all that was left was the heavy, scorched cinder of metal that we see today.

The third theory is that an ancient asteroid collision may have caused the small planet's very high proportions of metal. Computer simulations show that a blow from a large asteroid may have blasted off most of Mercury's less dense surface rock and rocky mantle. Finally, all that was left behind was its iron

A large asteroid (top) may have slammed into Mercury early in the planet's formation and stripped away all but its core of iron, a very heavy, dense metal (bottom).

Similarities between Earth's internal composition and Mercury's core are puzzling, since Mercury's surface (shown here) looks much more like the Moon's.

core. This theory may explain why measurements of Mercury's density are nearly as high as Earth's. That is, Mercury has nearly as much mass, or material, per unit of volume as Earth does. Yet on the surface, Mercury looks more like the Moon, which is much less dense. If Mercury once had more bulk, made of light materials, then its density may once have been much more like the Moon's.

Ancient Volcanic Action

New understanding of the *Mariner 10* pictures came when researchers compared pictures taken on Earth with the ones taken at Venus and Mercury. The science team studied samples of rock from the Moon in laboratories. They also compared how the Moon reflects light when seen through a telescope. They began to make some breakthroughs in understanding how the way you look at reflected light affects what you see. Then they applied color codes to different kinds of areas imaged by *Mariner*. They used color to enhance, or bring out, the difference in shapes on the planet's surface. Then they matched the color-enhanced map with other information they had gathered about the surface. From the combined facts, they could make some good guesses about the history of Mercury's interior. Their work has given new life and meaning to pictures that are nearly 30 years old.

These researchers have found some plains on Mercury that look a lot like lava plains on the Moon. Some of these areas are also not as heavily marked by craters as other regions of

The color enhancement added to this Mariner 10 image shows off Mercury's heavily pocked surface.

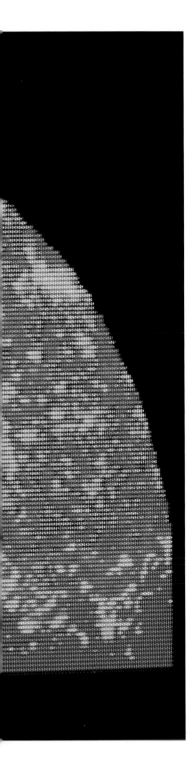

Mercury. Researchers think that ancient volcanoes may have erupted long ago and laid down lava beds. Some of these volcanoes may even have erupted after some of the worst smash hits took place during the early formation of the solar system some 3 to 4 billion years ago. Some of the plains, though, are probably not caused by volcanoes. Instead, they were most likely caused by heavy rains of dust and rock fragments after a large rock slammed into Mercury's surface.

Scientists need more information to be sure. Does Mercury's past include a story of violent volcanoes and a surface seething in molten lava? Also, what other facts can scientists discover about Mercury? Why is its core so large? Many mysteries about Mercury's interior remain for us to explore.

Much about Mercury remains a puzzle.

Chapter Five

Mercury's Mysteries

The little planet Mercury, traveling so close to the Sun, can give scientists an unusual window on the early solar system and how it formed. Understanding Mercury will help unlock many mysteries about the history of the four rocky planets. Scientists also still have a lot to learn about how magnetic fields are formed. They want to know more about volcanoes and their role in how the planets developed. Mercury's scarred face raises many questions—such as what kind of object could have created Caloris Basin? Mercury beckons with many questions, and the possibility for some new and better answers. And we have only seen one side so far!

Taking Another Look

When NASA launched its "great observatory" called the Hubble Space Telescope in 1990, it gave astronomers a clearer eye to see with. Positioned above the blur of Earth's atmosphere, the telescope would be an ideal tool for discovering more about Mercury. However, Mercury orbits too close to the Sun for safe observation by Hubble's sensitive instruments. So, the best way to find out answers to these and other questions is to go back for another look.

Scientists at NASA are working on a new mission to Mercury that may help answer some of these questions. Its name is MESSENGER—a good name for a mission to a planet named after Roman mythology's messenger to the gods. The name stands for *ME*rcury Surface, *S*pace *EN*vironment, *GE*ochemistry and *R*anging mission. The plan calls for launching the mission in 2004. After flying by Venus twice in 2007, MESSENGER should begin to orbit Mercury for one Earth-year in 2009. MESSENGER will set out to answer some of the basic questions raised by *Mariner 10*. It will try to answer the mystery of why Mercury is so dense. It will also explore the geologic history of Mercury. So far, exploration has covered only half the planet! What's on the other side?

Astronauts aboard the space shuttle update the Hubble Space Telescope's equipment on a maintenance mission in December 1999.

MESSENGER will try to find out if volcanoes have played as important a part in creating the plains as many scientists think. This mission will also try to find out more about whether Mercury's core is liquid or solid and how a planet so small can have a magnetic field. MESSENGER is also designed to examine the magnetic field and find out about its dynamics. Finally, MESSENGER planners hope to find out answers about the bright areas at Mercury's poles. Does this fiery hot planet harbor crystals of ice in shadowed craters at its poles? It takes a long time to plan and complete a mission to a planet, and scientists and engineers are already hard at work on it. Hopes are high that it will answer some of Mercury's many mysteries.

Two other space agencies are also planning missions to Mercury soon. Japan's national space research center, the Institute of Space and Aeronautical Science (ISAS), is planning a mission to Mercury to be launched in 2005. It should fly by Mercury once in 2008 and then return for an extended orbit in 2009. This mission is focusing on Mercury's internal structure and the makeup of the planet, especially its large iron core. It will also measure the magnetosphere, the area around Mercury that is affected by the planet's magnetic field. The spacecraft may also carry a probe that would gather information about the planet's surface. By the time the ISAS mission arrives in orbit around Mercury in 2009, the European Space Agency (ESA) hopes to launch its mission to Mercury, named BepiColombo. This mission has three parts.

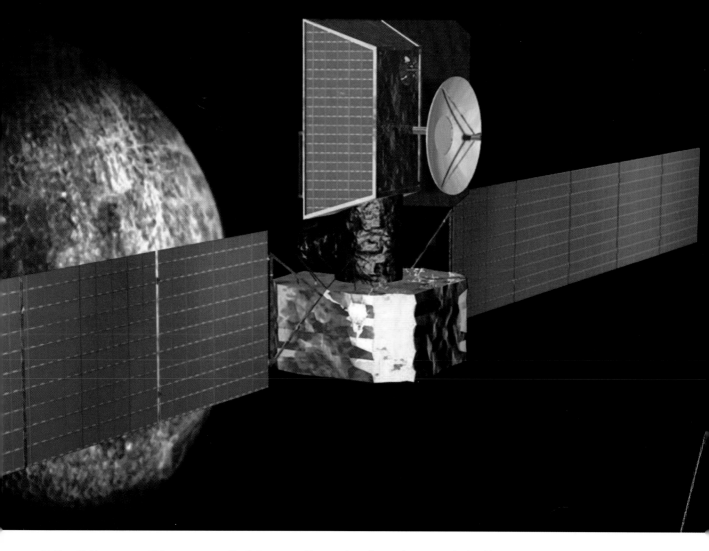

The Mercury Planetary Orbiter will study the planet globally. The Mercury Magnetosphere Orbiter will focus on the magnetosphere. The last piece, the Mercury Surface Element will land on the surface, or possibly bury itself in the surface, to explore its characteristics. If all goes well, we will know a lot more about the innermost planet by the end of the first decade of the 21st century.

Mercury is a world of many mysteries. Its position so close to the Sun has always made this planet difficult to study. Yet,

The European Space Agency (ESA) plans on launching BepiColombo in 2009.

Future missions to Mercury may help us understand how our solar system was formed.

thanks largely to the *Mariner 10* mission, scientists have found it is a place full of many surprises and stunning contrasts. The more we discover, the more questions we have—questions whose answers could unlock more mysteries about our solar system and the way it formed. In its innermost position in the solar system, Mercury is, as one scientist points out, an important little world.

Glossary

asteroid—a large rock that orbits the Sun and formed at the same time as the Sun and planets

atmosphere—the gases that surround a planet or other body in space.

axis—the imaginary line running from pole to pole through a planet's center. The planet spins, or rotates, along its axis.

comet—a small ball of rock and ice that orbits the Sun. When a comet approaches the Sun, some of the ice melts and releases gases. These gases form a tail behind the comet.

core—the hot, innermost region of a planet

crater—an irregular oval-shaped depression, or basin, created by a collision with another object

crust—the outer surface of a planet or moon

diameter—the length of a straight line through the center of an object

elliptical—oval-shaped

gravity—the force that pulls objects toward the center of a planet or other body in space

magnetometer—an instrument used to measure the strength of a magnetic field

mantle—a geologically different region below the crust of a planet, located between the crust and the core

mass—a grouping of matter with no particular shape

meteoroid—a rocky or metallic object of relatively small size, usually once part of a comet or asteroid

orbit—the path followed by one object moving around another object in space

revolution—one complete trip around the Sun

rotate—to turn or spin around a central point

solar nebula—the giant cloud of gases and dust from which the Sun and the planets were formed

thermal—involving heat

To Find Out More

Books

The news from space changes quickly, so it's always a good idea to check the copyright date on books to make sure that you are reading current information.

Brimner, Larry Dane. *Mercury*. New York: Children's Press, 1998.

Campbell, Ann Jeanette. *The New York Public Library Amazing Space: A Book of Answers for Kids*. New York: John Wiley & Sons, 1997.

Daily, Robert. *Mercury*. (First Books: The Solar System Series). New York: Franklin Watts, 1996.

Dickinson, Terence. *Other Worlds: A Beginner's Guide to Planets and Moons*. Willowdale, Ontario: Firefly Books, 1995.

Hartmann, William K. and Don Miller. *The Grand Tour.* New York: Workman Publishing, 1993.

Simon, Seymour. *Mercury.* New York: William Morrow & Co., 1998.

Vogt, Gregory L. *Mercury.* Brookfield, Conn.: Millbrook Press, 1998.

————. *The Solar System: Facts and Exploration.* Scientific American Sourcebooks. New York: Twenty-First Century Books, 1995.

CD-ROM

Beyond Planet Earth
For Macintosh and PC (DOS, Windows, OS2). From the Discovery Channel School Multimedia. An interactive journey to the planets, including Mercury. Includes video from NASA and *Voyager* missions and more than 200 photographs. Discovery Channel School, P.O. Box 970, Oxon Hill, MD 20750-0970; Phone: 888-892-3494; Fax: 301-567-9553

Video

Discover Magazine: Solar System
Discovery Channel School, P.O. Box 970, Oxon Hill, MD 20750-0970

Organizations and Online Sites

These organizations and groups are good sources of information about Mercury and the rest of the solar system. Many of the online sites listed below are NASA sites, with links to many other interesting sources of information.

NASA Ask a Space Scientist
http://image.gsfc.nasa.gov/poetry/ask/askmag.html#list
Interactive page where NASA scientists answer your questions about astronomy, space, and space missions. Also has archives and fact sheets

The Nine Planets: A Multimedia Tour of the Solar System
http://www.seds.org/nineplanets/nineplanets/nineplanets.html
Includes excellent material on Mercury and other planets from the Students for the Exploration and Development of Space, University of Arizona.

Planetary Missions
http://nssdc.gsfc.nasa.gov/planetary/projects.html
Page of NASA links to all of current and past missions, a one-stop shopping center to a wealth of information

The Planetary Society
65 North Catalina Avenue
Pasadena, CA 91106-2301
http://www.planetary.org/

Sky Online

http://www.skypub.com

The web site for *Sky and Telescope* magazine and other publications of Sky Publishing Corporation. This site has a good weekly news section on general space and astronomy news. The site also contains many good tips for amateur astronomers, as well as a helpful selection of links. A list of science museums, planetariums, and astronomy clubs organized by state helps locate nearby places to visit, as well.

Welcome to the Planets

http://pds.jpl.nasa.gov/planets/

Tour of the solar system with lots of pictures and information. Created by California Institute of Technology for NASA/Jet Propulsion Laboratory.

Windows to the Universe

http://windows.arc.nasa.gov/

NASA site, developed by the University of Michigan, includes sections on "Our Planet," "Our Solar System," "Space Missions," and "Kids' Space." Choose from presentation levels of beginner, intermediate, or advanced. To begin exploring, go to the URL above and choose "Enter the Site."

A Note on Sources

When we write about space science, we like to find the most up-to-date sources we can because scientists keep finding out more about the universe. We read as many of the latest books as we can find. (You should see our library—wall-to-wall books!) We find recent articles in science magazines such as *Scientific American* and *Science News*. We also use the Internet a lot. The National Aeronautics and Space Administration (NASA) keeps us up-to-date by e-mailing us the latest reports from scientists who study the data from spacecraft. We also check the NASA web pages (such as those listed at the end of this book).

Our favorite kind of research involves talking with planetologists about what they love best—the work they are doing to discover more about our solar system and the universe. We would especially like to thank our editor Tara Moncrief and

Sam Storch, Lecturer at the American Museum-Hayden Planetarium, who reviewed the manuscript and made many excellent suggestions.

—*Ray Spangenburg and Kit Moser*

Index

Numbers in *italics* indicate illustrations.

NASA, 17, 48
Neptune, *15*, 16

Orbit, 7, 8, 16, 35

Planets, 12
   formation of, 6–8, 47
   "missing", 16
   moonless, 8
   "rocky," 39, 47
   in solar system, *14–15*

Radar, 13, 24
Revolution, 7
Roman mythology, 6
Rotate, 7, 13, 23

Saturn, 6, *15*
Schiaparelli, Giovanni, *10*, 11–12
Solar nebula, 6, 40
Solar system
   "great bombardment" theory, 7, 28
   origin of, 6–7, 28, 45, 47
   picture of, *14–15*
South Pole-Aitken Basin, 30
Spacecraft
   Clementine, 25

Lunar Prospector, 25
Mariner 10 spacecraft, 17, *18*, 19–26, 27, 29, 32, 38, *38*, 39, 43, *44*, 48, 52
MESSENGER, 48–50
Sun, in relation to Mercury, *4*, 5, 8, 12, 13, *14*, 16–17, 51
Surface of Mercury. *See also* Caloris Basin; Crater
   figuring out age of, 33–35
   photos of, *4, 21, 22, 24, 26, 29, 31, 33, 34, 38, 42, 44, 46, 52*

Tectonics, 30
Telescope, 10, 11, 43, 48, *49*
Thermal, 33
Titan (moon), 6

Ultraviolet (UV) spectrometer, 20

Venus, 8–9, *9*, *15*, 17, 39, 43
Volcano, 8, 34, 38, 45, 47, 50
Vulcan, 16

About the Authors

Ray Spangenburg and Kit Moser write together about science and technology. This husband-and-wife writing team has written 38 books and more than 100 articles. Their works include a five-book series on the history of science and a series on space exploration and astronomy. Their writing has taken them on some great adventures. They have flown on NASA's Kuiper Airborne Observatory (a big plane carrying a telescope). They have also visited the Deep Space Network in the Mojave Desert, where signals from spacecraft are collected. They have even flown in zero gravity on an experimental NASA flight. Ray and Kit live and write in Carmichael, California, with their two dogs, Mencken (a Sharpei mix) and F. Scott Fitz (a Boston terrier).